To my hubby
With love and Thanks
for our Arizona Move.

The best from
ARIZONA
HIGHWAYS

by Tom C. Cooper

designed by Laurie Cook

Storm clouds hover over the Grand Canyon.
Darwin Van Campen

Published by *Arizona Highways*, 2039 West Lewis Avenue, Phoenix, Arizona 85009 U.S.A. James E. Stevens, Director of Publications, Department of Transportation, State of Arizona. Joseph Stacey, Editor. Typography by Morneau Typographers, Phoenix, Arizona. Printed by W. A. Krueger Company, Phoenix, Arizona.

"Pima Indian Drummer Boy."
Ted DeGrazia

Cover Photo — Winter comes to the Grand Canyon.
Dick Dietrich

contents

Sunrise reflections.

Earl Petroff

preface

Assembling photographs and art for a book representing *The Best from Arizona Highways* is an awesome, but exciting experience. At times the project seemed impossible because of the great quantity of outstanding visual material which has appeared in the magazine during its first 50 years.

But it would be regrettable for a magazine, internationally recognized as a scenic showpiece for Arizona and the Southwest, to celebrate a half century of publishing without collecting the most memorable photographs and art into a single volume.

So this commemorative book just had to be.

An initial selection of nearly 1,100 color illustrations was made. This number was edited down to 315. Eventually, a most difficult decision was reached — approximately 160 would be published.

The selection of content was the sole responsibility of this writer. Criteria were, first, to choose photographs and art which had the greatest *visual impact*, and second, to select material which represented a *variety* of Arizona and Southwestern subjects (it is possible to select from the pages of *Arizona Highways* more than one hundred dramatic photographs of the Grand Canyon alone).

Regardless of the criteria used, and the care and diligence one might exert in choosing content, it is logical to expect disagreement.

After having repeatedly probed bound volumes and single copies of the magazine over a three-year period, I came away from the experience overwhelmed by the tremendous quantity of superb visual material. Perhaps "visually numbed" is a better description.

It would be easy to credit nature for the subject matter and technology for the manner in which it was portrayed, and then stop there. But it has taken *people* to make *Arizona Highways*...many of them.

Editors, writers, photographers, artists, and directors; accountants, circulation staff, record-keepers, receptionists, mailers, secretaries, and clerks; engravers, typesetters, printers and pressmen...have loved the magazine, nurtured it, babied it, so that readers around the world would be assured of their copy.

This volume is dedicated to these many people.

Tom C. Cooper
Tucson, Arizona

Summer sunset on Canyon Lake.

David Muench

The classics

The best from

The Superstition Mountains and a desert mood.
Esther Henderson

The pace-setter of visual magazines.
The most beautiful thing in the mail.
The granddaddy of pictorial magazines.

A tradition in the magazine industry.

These are statements from readers, magazine industry executives, and historians describing *Arizona Highways.*

The magazine has attained an international reputation for excellence in portraying the scenery and people of Arizona and the Southwest. The reputation has grown steadily as editors have become more artful in selecting visual content, as photographers and artists have developed greater skill and insight into their subjects, and as photographic and printing technology have advanced.

In its first 600 editions, covering a half century, enough memorable and dramatic images have appeared in *Arizona Highways* to overpower even the most visually sophisticated reader. Obviously, some of the photos rank as outstanding. One might call them "classics" or the "best of best." An attempt has been made to assemble these "classics" in this first chapter. For sure, such an effort will bring out controversy, prejudices, favorites, and probably the rhetorical question, "How dare anyone attempt it?" But it has been attempted as a visual tribute to the people and the subject matter which have made *Arizona Highways.*

The magazine, born in 1925, began using photography sparingly. The first photos were uninspiring black and white scenes of road construction, bridges — even culverts. After all, *the magazine was a highway department publication intended to promote Arizona roads!* By 1935, the black and white photos began to improve technically. Perhaps more significantly, subject matter increased in interest. Instead of showing a new cut through a mountain or ridge, there were canyons. Instead of a new highway maintenance shop, there were 18th century missions. And cowboys, gunslingers, desert spas, Indian ceremonials, and sunsets.

A summer forest and morning shadows.
Willis Peterson

Ray Manley

Moonlight and cowboys.

In July, 1938, the first color photograph appeared, on the cover, depicting the red rock formations of Oak Creek Canyon. It was remarkable by 1938 standards and is even "good" by today's technology.

A few months later, the editor announced a photography contest to "show off Arizona," with prizes awarded in the amount of $15, $10 and $5.

The mold was taking shape. *Arizona Highways* was becoming a visual publication.

Late afternoon sun and gold.
David Muench

Navajo child and friend, Monument Valley. *Ray Manley*

The preceding panel —
Weather, sunlight and the Grand Canyon.
David Muench

The desert greets a sunrise.
David Muench

But there was also advertising. It did little to enhance the verbal and visual content of the fledgling magazine. It annoyed editor Raymond Carlson. Coincidentally, a highway commissioner, Jack Proctor of Tucson, approached Carlson with a new plan — make *Arizona Highways* a tourist promotion magazine. *"Fill it with pictures of Arizona's scenery"* was the mandate.

Proctor promised Carlson additional state finances to expand the magazine. The legislature responded. In February, 1939, the last advertisement appeared.

The modern *Arizona Highways* was born. The magazine would extol the virtues of Arizona's scenery in color photography. And without commercial distractions.

Things began to happen. From a miniscule state highway department promotion piece, with circulation hovering around ten to twenty thousand, the magazine began to blossom, and then reached full bloom following World War II. Circulation reached an all-time high in January, 1974, when nearly a million copies were printed and sold of the now famous "turquoise issue." But it took more than a change in policy on advertising and the development of good color photographic materials to make *Arizona Highways* what it is today. Three additional elements came together at about the same time.

Editor Raymond Carlson was not even a snap-shot photographer, but he knew good photography when he saw it and he knew how to publish it. Josef Muench, Esther Henderson and other photographers located Carlson in an old adobe office building in Phoenix and presented him with dramatic and memorable color photos of Arizona. Printing technology also advanced to the point where you could print reasonably good color.

A Navajo family and flock in Monument Valley.   Josef Muench

The four came together — the right elements at the right time.

The good photography came in slowly at first. But soon, talented photographers by the dozens began to beat a path to the editor's door... not for the pay they might receive, but for the opportunity of seeing their work printed in *Arizona Highways.*

Today, there are those who say, "Every photograph printed in *Arizona Highways* is a classic." Well maybe. Perhaps it depends on your definition. Webster defines a classic as, "A work...of the highest class and of acknowledged excellence." Taking that as a criterion, then *Arizona Highways* has had its share of "classics," and then some.

Navajos and their flock,
Monument Valley.
Josef Muench

15

What makes a classic scenic photograph? Perhaps you could produce such a photograph with luck alone. But luck is a fleeting thing and it belongs more to the gambling world than photography.

What then does it take to produce an *Arizona Highways* classic?

Technical competence — a mastery of camera and related equipment, film and darkroom techniques.

Visual training — a deep understanding of composition and form; how a scene looks under certain lighting or atmospheric conditions, and finding that viewpoint which best serves the subject and reader.

Timing — yes, luck, to some degree. But more importantly, knowing when the lighting will be right, when to expect snow or fog, or golden leaves, or cactus in bloom. That's timing.

Persistence — going back time and again, over rough roads, or no roads at all, for that right moment.

Sacrifice — missing meals, getting up before sunrise, weathering out a storm, plodding through snow, sweating out a desert day, sleeping on the ground, traveling, and traveling.

Dedication — the financial rewards are not great, but the photographers realize that before clicking the shutter. There's something else. Do the job well, don't let the editors and readers down. Do justice to the subject.

Arizona Highways does *not* have a staff of dozens of talented photographers. It does not have even *one* staff photographer. In the history of the magazine only one man has been listed as such (Norman Wallace, prior to World War II). Instead, the editors have relied on freelance amateur and professional photographers for contributions.

But the submissions have poured in, by the tens of thousands — perhaps by the hundreds of thousands. Many of the frequently published photographers, some of them internationally known, look to *Arizona Highways* first when they have good material. They know that the editors will appreciate it and will use it well. They know that technically, it will be published by the most sophisticated and skilled processes available to the publishing industry.

That is loyalty and respect. Loyalty to the magazine and its readers. Respect for the reputation which the magazine has earned.

These are the things of which *Arizona Highways* classics are made.

*A brilliant sunrise
brings a new day
to the Grand
Canyon.*
Josef Muench

The following panel —

**Navajo sentries in
Monument Valley.**
Ray Manley

*The last rays
of a winter day.*
Don Valentine

*A bouquet of
blooming yuccas.*
Darwin Van Campen

Mission San Xavier del Bac radiates in the night.
David Muench

The face of Tumacacori Mission.
Darwin Van Campen

orches in the desert.
David Muench

Fall lingers along an Arizona stream.
David Muench

A morning mist hangs over the Mogollon Rim.
Dick Dietrich

The day is over.

Ray Manley

indian land

A Navajo in his land, Monument Valley.   Ray Manley

ndian land in Arizona means vast areas, some of them known the world over for spectacular views, color and natural phenomena. Indian land also means people — the enduring natives who have populated the area for centuries.

The scenery consists of spires, buttes, mesas, canyons, forests and desert vistas. Time has changed it slowly. Rock formations are carved by the elements. Sand drifts into patterns, erases itself, then drifts back again. Plant life has evolved gradually, learning to adjust to the subtle changes in climate. Leaves have evolved into thorny spines on the cactus; other plants have evolved into bizarre forms and life cycles. Animal life also has learned to cope with the land. The strongest have survived.

Change has, indeed, come very gradually.

And so it is with the people — Apaches, Navajos, Hopis, Papagos and others. They have changed over the centuries, but very slowly.

Today these people possess a quiet charm — and determination, strength and durability. Many of them cling to old customs and beliefs, language and dress. They add a stability and uniqueness to the land that is theirs.

Indian land in Arizona means 20 million acres, nearly 27 percent of the state's land area. There are 17 reservations scattered about the state, occupied by 14 different tribes.

Cattle raising in Monument Valley.
Carlos Elmer

Joy Navasie (Frog Woman) in her Hopi corn field surrounded by examples of her art.

Ray Manley Studios

Winter moves in on a Navajo hogan in Canyon de Chelly.

David Muench

The Navajo Reservation, in the northeast quadrant of Arizona, is the largest with nearly 9 million acres or 25,000 square miles. The Navajo lands, edging into Utah on the north, and into New Mexico on the east, occupy an area larger than West Virginia or about as large as Connecticut, Delaware, Maryland, Massachusetts and Rhode Island combined.

Some of the nation's most dramatic scenery is within the tribe's boundaries — Monument Valley, Canyon de Chelly, and nearby, the Grand Canyon and Lake Powell. The land is diverse, ranging from pine-covered mountains visited early by snow, to the barren red sandstone of Monument Valley dotted with spires and buttes. It is perhaps the most photographed Indian land in the world.

It is also the land of a colorful and gifted people. There are approximately 75,000 Navajos living on the reservation in Arizona. They are known the world over for their silversmithing and weaving.

In the middle of the Navajo reservation are lands of the Hopi, a pueblo or village tribe numbering about 7,000 people. The Hopis are deeply religious, mostly agrarian, and are skilled artisans with pottery, basket weaving and silver. They live in several villages on or near mesas. Old Oraibi, one of their settlements, is believed to be the oldest, continuously inhabited village in North America, dating back to 1,200 A.D. or earlier.

"Faith and Hope." Courtesy of
Mr. and Mrs. Virgil Gerig.
James Abeita

Bob Bradshaw

Herding the flock in Navajoland.

The Apache is the second largest tribe in Arizona in land holdings and numbers of people. The tribal lands are in east-central Arizona, encompassing 3.5 million acres divided into two reservations — the Fort Apache and San Carlos. There are approximately 12,000 Apaches living on the two reservations. Their livelihood is chiefly forestry and ranching.

The Papagos are the largest of several desert-dwelling tribes. Their land consists of 2.8 million acres stretching from the Mexican border Southwest of Tucson to an area halfway to Phoenix. There are nearly 9,000 members in the tribe. Basket weaving is a special craft of the Papago, but cattle raising is the tribe's chief source of income.

Neighbors of the Papago are the desert-dwelling Pimas and Maricopas, residing south and east of Phoenix. The combined population of the two tribes is about 11,000.

Residing on the western edges of Arizona are the Cocopahs and the Yumas in the Yuma area near the Colorado River. Located to the north along the river area are three small tribes — the Chemehuevi, Mohave and Hualapai. The Yavapai are found near the city of Prescott. And the Paiute on the Arizona-Utah border north of the Grand Canyon.

The Havasupai is one of the state's smallest tribes. However, the Supai people (the Anglo added "Hava," meaning water) occupy one of the most remote villages in the continental United States. The tribe survives on approximately 3,000 acres about 2,000 feet below the rim of the Grand Canyon. Access to the village is limited to hiking, horseback or helicopter. The tribe numbers less than 400 and supports its members by farming and packing visitors down the winding eight-mile trail.

Nearly all of Arizona's Indian people share two common environmental problems — a lack of water and a shortage of building materials. Yet they have endured. The Navajo, numbering only about 16,000 a century ago, now are more than 100,000 strong living in the three-state reservation area of Arizona, New Mexico and Utah. Most other tribes are holding their own in numbers.

A family's livelihood, Monument Valley.
Josef Muench

Portrait of a Hopi Harvest Dancer.
Esther Henderson

The preceding panel —
An outdoor studio in Monument Valley.
Josef Muench

The following panel —
The eternal mittens, Monument Valley.
Ray Manley

"Coyote," a Navajo man, by Adam Clark Vroman,
photographed on the Navajo Reservation in 1901.
From the collection of William Webb.

Sand painting in Monument Valley to bring health to a patient.
Josef Muench

"*Navajo Girl and Goats.*" *Courtesy of Husberg's Fine Art Gallery.*
Ray Swanson

Light, shadow, sand and composition, Monument Valley.
Allen C. Reed

Allen C. Reed

Sky, rock and dunes, Monument Valley.

There is another problem common to all of Arizona's Indians. Many young people leave the reservation for education in nearby towns, and some join the military service and see vast areas of the world. It is agonizing to tribal elders that some of these young people choose not to return to the reservation as nurses, teachers, artists and businessmen. However, the reservation is a magnet for many of these young people. They return to find conditions much the same as when they left — a shortage of firewood, few job opportunities, poor health conditions and a lack of adequate housing. The many who do return become involved in tribal customs, ceremonies and political action. It offers them hope and peace.

Tribal life usually hangs in a delicate balance influenced by today's social problems, devastating rains or snow, drought and prolonged periods of cold or heat. They live with the land, and with their beliefs, religion and an indestructible will to be a proud and resourceful people.

The Navajos call themselves *Dineh* or *Dine*, meaning the people. They and other Arizona Indians are — *the* people.

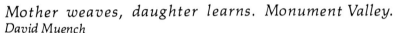

Mother weaves, daughter learns. Monument Valley.
David Muench

Agatha Peak, a background for a Navajo home.

David Muench

A Navajo views her world.
Ray Manley

Apache cowboys.
Herb and Dorothy McLaughlin

The following panel —
Sandstone monuments, Navajoland.
David Muench

"Apache Warrior."
Ted De Grazia

57

Joseph Lonewolf.
Ray Manley Studios

A Papago mother harvests fruit of the saguaro.
Western Ways

The following panel —
The grandeur of Havasu Falls.
Ray Manley

60

Home of the ancient ones, Cliff Palace, Mesa Verde National Park, Colorado.

Josef Muench

"Alice Lee Etsitty." Courtesy of Husberg's Fine Arts Gallery.   Ray Swanson

Weather moves in on Monument Valley.

Herb and Dorothy McLaughlin

"Smile pretty, please."
Esther Henderson

Following their shadows home.

David Muench

Young mother and child.
J. H. McGibbeny

The preceding panel —
"Navajo Night Chant."
Ted De Grazia

The following panel —
Monument Valley from the rim.
David Muench

Pueblo Bonito Ruins.
David Muench

"Navajo." Courtesy of Troy's Cowboy Art Gallery.

Robert Rishell

"Desert Hill" — Navajo woman.
Ansel Adams

"Three Little Apaches Waiting."

Ted De Grazia

Hopi potter.
J. H. McGibbeny

"Little Papago."   Ted De Grazia

"Navajo Bride."   Ted De Grazia

Winter hogan, Navajoland.
Arthur A. Twomey

Allen C. Reed

Apache cattle country.

The epitome of craftsmanship —
Silver jewel box with Morenci turquoise.
The necklace of Zuni fetish is strung with
turquoise beads. Kachina Traders/Private Collection
Peter L. Bloomer Photo

The harvest is in. Time to move.
Bob Bradshaw

The following panel —
A Navajo paints with sand.
Ray Manley

The preceding panel —
Nature's sculpture.
David Muench

Sunrise in Monument Valley.
Carlos Elmer

Late day in Monument Valley.

Dick Dietrich

A proud Navajo surveys his land.

Ray Manley

"Navajo Wagon Race."

Ted De Grazia

Salado Ruins, home of the early ones.
David Muench

Taos Pueblo, New Mexico.
David Muench

"Navajo Madonna." Courtesy of Mrs. Olaf Wieghorst Collection.   *Olaf Wieghorst*

THE DESERT

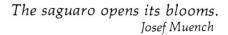

The saguaro opens its blooms.
Josef Muench

View into Peralta Canyon.
David Muench

people coming to the desert for the first time from other parts of the country are sometimes shocked. Their experience has not prepared them for the strange and bizarre region that is the Sonoran Desert of Arizona and northern Mexico.

Many first see this desert from the air, or a fast moving train or car. Their remarks are frequently unflattering, even brutal. To dwellers or friends of the desert the reaction is expected, and understood.

From the perspective of a freeway or airway the desert *is* uninviting, harsh, desolate — a place to pass over or get through. "Even God was unkind to this land," many will say.

The term *desert* means an arid region. Its Latin derivation means *abandoned* or *deserted*. Arid it is, for some parts of the desert get less than five inches of moisture annually. But the desert is not abandoned or deserted. It abounds with life.

For centuries, the Pima, Papago, Yuma and other Indian tribes have endured the Arizona desert. They have learned to respect it, and to *live* on this land. It is their home. Few members of these desert tribes leave their reservation for very long. There is *something* about this land that brings them back. That *something* you don't see from overhead or from a fast moving vehicle on the freeways.

That *something* takes sharp eyes to see. It takes knowing, time, and patience. That *something* can grow on you.

Photographers and writers who have become regular contributors to *Arizona Highways* magazine have found that *something*. For fifty years they have photographed and written about the desert — and they have given the world an intimate view of this unusual environment.

Esther Henderson

Long shadows — White Sands National Monument, New Mexico.

Red hedgehog cactus.
John Candelario

A desert rainbow and a stormy sky.
Western Ways

Bright winter day in the desert.

Ray Manley

First, there is the strange world of the cactus. The word is from Greek *(kaktos)* meaning a prickly plant with thick, fleshy stems, usually with no leaves and having a heavy cluster of thorns. It has adapted itself to thrive in hot, dry climates. It has armed itself to survive long periods of drought, and has clothed itself in spiny armor for protection against animal life which might desire its succulent interior.

The giant saguaro (pronounced *sa-war-oo*), the monarch of the Arizona desert, employs a very shallow, wide-spreading root system to gather in the sporadic and limited moisture. The body or main trunk of the cactus is pleated and can expand considerably to accommodate moisture storage. In dry periods, the reservoir of water inside the trunk is gradually used up, and the girth of the cactus gradually shrinks, until another rain, at which time the saguaro again draws up its supply of water.

Newcomers to the desert are always amazed at the ease with which cactus can be transplanted. A branch from a cholla or prickly pear cactus can fall to the ground, and even if left untouched for days or weeks, will send down roots and re-establish itself from the moisture and strength within.

Prickly pear cactus in bloom.
Josef Muench

Nature is the artist.

Willis Peterson

Thelocactus bicolor.
John Candelario

Stately saguaro cactus against the Santa Catalina Mountains near Tucson.
Josef Muench

Grass trails near Wickenburg.
David Muench

A Tucson family enjoys twilight.
Ray Manley

The torches of spring.   *Darwin Van Campen*

A myriad of animals and reptiles thrive in the desert environment. To passing visitors, they may go totally unnoticed. Take for example a hot summer day on the desert. It is time for rest and quiet. At high noon, with air temperatures ranging from 105 to 120 degrees, and ground temperatures up to 160 degrees, the desert appears empty of life, except for the vegetation which stands defiantly. But on the ground and beneath it, and under the shade of shrubs and trees, there rests a complex and unusual world of wildlife.

So to pass through the desert on a searing summer day is to find it seemingly lifeless. The birds are quiet. Nothing moves unless forced into activity. Perhaps a bundle of tumbleweed may be kicked along by a breeze. And here and there one might spot a *dust-devil*, miniature cyclones or tornadoes common in the desert. The rest of the land is waiting.

But to visit the desert at dusk is to see it come alive. Birds move and become noisy, reptiles awaken, coyotes roam and here and there one can see small animals darting around.

Even the menacing-looking spines of cactus take on a softer, more hospitable look as they pick up the warm glow of the setting sun. It is truly a different desert... one that captures people, or brings them back time and again. It is a desert throbbing with life. It is alive, and friendly.

Desert beauty.
R. C. and Claire Meyer Proctor

Cholla cactus in sunlight.
David Muench

Summer excitement on the desert.
Tom Carroll

Brooding mountains on the desert.

R. H. Wahlgren

Snowball cactus.
John Candelario

A desert afternoon.
Carlos Elmer

A soft moment at the end of day.
Harry Vroman

Owls come home to the saguaro cactus.
Don Bleitz

The winds of time shape the earth.
Willis Peterson

There are those who say the desert is worthless. "You can't grow anything but cactus there," some say. However, some of the richest and most productive soils on earth are found in Arizona's Salt River Valley, Casa Grande Valley, the Valley of the Santa Cruz, and the lands around Yuma and Parker. These are, or rather were, desert areas. Man has learned to add *moisture*, by means of irrigation, and turned these desert soils into highly productive agricultural regions.

Add moisture to almost any desert slope or valley and watch the area spring to life with poppies, hedgehog or pincushion cactus, and the magnificent display of yellow from the palo verde tree. Or look in another direction and see great fields of lettuce, or groves of citrus.

Visit the desert at the right hour and you will see a striking display of animal life.

Truly, the desert is a verdant land, which can come to life under the right conditions of moisture and temperature. It is just waiting for the patient and observant person to appreciate it.

This chapter puts the living desert on display as seen through the eyes and lenses of photographers who have become intimate with the moods and whims of this remarkable region.

A carpet of golden poppies cover an Arizona hillside.
David Muench

A moonrise greets a desert slope.
Tom C. Cooper

Close-up of hedgehog cactus.
John Candelario

Desert reflections after a rain.
Bob Riddell

A spring display of desert claret cups (hedgehog cactus).
Josef Muench

Springtime near the Superstition Mountains.
Josef Muench

Setting sun in saguaroland.
David Muench

The giants of the desert stand stoically on an Arizona hillside.
Ray Manley

The road across no-man's land, Panamint Valley, California.   Esther Henderson

A crown of blossoms graces a barrel cactus.
Josef Muench

Sunrise silhouette.
Earl Petroff

The following panel —
Flowering yuccas and a moon over the desert.
Josef Muench

The canyons

It is by design that the canyons of Arizona and southern Utah appear frequently in vibrant color in *Arizona Highways*. The editors have known that the Grand Canyon, for example, is the nation's most popular scenic attraction and have used her regularly to grace the pages of the magazine. It is a fact, too, that more words have appeared in the magazine on the Grand and other canyons than any other subject. Many of these have been technical descriptions of the canyon's exploration, geologic significance, or size.

In the case of the Grand Canyon, editors have turned to photography to show the lavishly rich coloration, the formidably sculptured formations, the breath-taking gorges or the sheerness of the walls. This paragraph proves the inadequacy of explaining the visual drama of the Grand Canyon. Description simply fails, as was aptly pointed out by the renowned author Frank Waters. In his book, *The Colorado*, Waters wrote: *No writer of worth has ever seriously attempted to describe Grand Canyon; no artist has ever adequately portrayed it. None ever will.*

Yet editors and readers alike thirst for the visual excitement unique to the canyons. In its first fifty years of publishing, *Arizona Highways* has shown a Grand Canyon scene on the cover 30 times — once every 20 months on the average..

The wayward Colorado River, Canyonlands National Park, Utah.

Esther Henderson

Snow adds a new dimension to Bryce Canyon National Park, Utah.

Allen C. Reed

The following panel —
A summer storm engulfs the grandest canyon of them all.
Esther Henderson

127

White velvet covers the Grand Canyon. *Ray Manley*

It might also be true that the Grand Cayon has been singularly the most professionally photographed attraction in the nation. Josef Muench, the dean of contributing photographers to *Arizona Highways*, has made approximately 180 trips to the Grand Canyon to capture her beauty and moods.

Let's explore briefly some facts about this grandest of all canyons and the challenge it presents to the photographer and artist.

The Grand Canyon has been developing for several millions of years, perhaps as many as ten. It is a mile deep in most places. It is 200 miles long, and from four to 18 miles wide. The area represents numerous climatic zones. The north rim, the highest at 8200 feet above sea level, gets approximately 26 inches of moisture annually. Vegetation is forest-like — spruce, fir and aspens. The south rim is 7000 feet and receives nearly 15 inches of moisture a year. Major vegetation is small pine and juniper. The bottom of the canyon, at the river level, averages about 2500 feet, and one finds a desert environment — cacti and agave plants.

The following panel —
A rainbow and a threatening storm hover over Canyon de Chelly.
Lengendary Spider Rock in the foregound rises
several hundred feet from the canyon floor. *Willis Peterson*

Ground fog spills over the canyon rim.
James Tallon

Wildlife varies widely, from the north rim, to the bottom and back up to the south rim.

A durable hiker can hike down one rim and up the other side in a day and pass through climate, plant and animal life that represent most of the nation's extremes.

There is so much of everything — color, size, texture and variety. Where does one begin to photograph?

Size, distance and perspective are often lost because photographers, be they professional or amateur, frequently fail to utilize foreground as a reference point or as a frame. It is a tragedy to see visitors walk to a canyon rim at noon, snap a couple of pictures, shrug and walk away. You know they haven't really *seen* the canyon, be it Sabino, Aravaipa or the Grand. The disappointment is evident on their faces and on the film or print that results.

Photographers know best that to capture the splendor of the Grand Canyon or any other canyon, one must wait for the right moment. You must watch for shadows to deepen and become more intense to enhance the richness of the spectacularly colored rock formations. You might wait for weather to soften or intensify the harshness of the canyon. Or get up early and wait for the sun to sneak in over the canyon, or wait patiently for its last rays to linger at dusk.

The Grand Canyon is a multitude of moods changing with the seasons, the viewpoint, color of the rock, weather conditions and time of day. These scenes typify two of the moods.   David Muench

Sycamore Canyon panorama.

Ray Manley

A White Christmas among the Red Cliffs.
Ed Ellinger

Left — Sunset mood, the Grand Canyon.
David Muench

*Majestic White
House Ruins,
dating back to
1100 A.D. are
guarded by the
towering walls
of Canyon de Chelly.*
Bob Bradshaw

141

An aerial view of the downward cutting Colorado River and the rising Colorado Plateau north of the Grand Canyon.
Joe Maskasky

The following panel —
Eternal Castle Rock along Oak Creek.
Ray Manley

It is known that many respected professional photographers from various parts of the country have stopped at the canyons of the Southwest to meet the photographic challenge. These are highly qualified professionals, extremely skilled and experienced. Many of them have been disappointed with their results.

There is a reason. Josef and David Muench, Ray Manley, Esther Henderson, Darwin Van Campen, Willis Peterson and other *Arizona Highways* regulars have become intimate with these canyons, from above and below, in all seasons, and in all kinds of weather.

They have a rapport with the canyons developed over many years. It is evident in their work appearing in the magazine.

It is easy to believe that these brilliant photographers communicate with the canyons...and the canyons with them.

Judge for yourself.

The labyrinth at the bottom of the Grand Canyon.
David Muench

Sunset glow from Hopi Point, Grand Canyon.

Darwin Van Campen

THE SEASONS

The glow of a spring evening.　　　　　*James Tallon*

Some people won't believe it, but Arizona does have *four* seasons. Two and three may be apparent in various parts of the state at the same time. Altitude and latitude control a wide magnitude of climatic conditions. Spring may be in full bloom in one region, and another area may be under six to ten feet of snow. Swimming meets might flourish on a given Saturday in Yuma, Phoenix or Tucson, while in the higher elevations of the White Mountains, ice fishermen might be patiently waiting for a nibble.

Such is Arizona!

Spring comes early on the desert or low lands.　Winter rainfall, though it might be sparse, has left its strength for the desert vegetation. Let temperatures move into the seventies and eighties and the desert comes to life — flowers on ocotillo, poppies, saguaros and palo verdes.

But in the higher elevations and areas in between, spring comes slowly. The runoff starts. Skiing stops. The red sands of Monument Valley appear again from under frequent blankets of snow. Streams rush from the higher elevations. Reservoirs swell under the melting snow-pack in the mountains. The water is held at Saguaro, Canyon, Roosevelt, Apache and San Carlos lakes. The water will provide recreation at the reservoirs, domestic use in Maricopa County, and irrigation for farmers and ranchers.

It will mean a productive summer in an otherwise difficult land.

The following panel — A carpet of poppies.
David Muench

Spring comes to the Black Canyon of the Colorado River.
David Muench

148

Happy grazing in a summer meadow.   *Arthur Twomey*

Fishing for breakfast on Hawley Lake.   Bob Ratliffe

Summer!

In the low lands summer means taking that daily stroll early in the morning before temperatures move over a hundred. It means plenty of swimming, boating, sitting in the shade.

It also means getting up early, starting work at five-thirty, quitting at two.

For the Papago Indians summer means watching the fruit of the saguaro and keeping an eye on the water level at livestock watering tanks. Other cattlemen anxiously watch those thunderstorms that build up into dramatic threats...and frequently move on into other regions.

Away from the desert and a short distance into the low mountains streams are running. There's some fishing. Plenty of picnics. Hiking is good too. Try the golf at Flagstaff, Prescott, Tubac and the White Mountains.

It's time to roam in Arizona. Whenever possible livestock are moved to the higher, cooler and greener grazing lands. The people follow too, for that's where the campfires crackle on a cool summer evening, and the breezes are freshest.

That's summer in Arizona!

153

The Needles, upper Lake Havasu.

Carlos Elmer

A delicate perch.   James Tallon

The end of day.   *Darwin Van Campen*

A summer evening on a trail ride.
Peter Bloomer

Fall comes to Arizona...at different times. Elevation is the determining factor. Autumn is seen first on the North Rim of the Grand Canyon (8400 feet above sea level), in the White Mountains (7000 to 11,000) and around the San Francisco Peaks (12,000) near Flagstaff. It begins slowly with cooling evenings. Then frost moves into these areas and things begin to happen.

Autumn color!

A photographer can travel for three months in the state chasing the color as it moves from the higher elevations down to the lowest parts of the desert.

The aspens react first, turning to a delicate gold-yellow. Their leaves flutter, or quake — the symphony of autumn! Everyone loves this season. Air conditioners are turned down or off, and there is a feeling in Arizona that a fresh new season is here. For sure, it means relief for the desert dwellers. For others it is time to put on storm windows.

The fall color moves gradually down from the higher elevations into the Prescott, Payson and Sedona-Oak Creek areas.

One and two months later that same fall that started in Arizona's high country in late September has reached grassland areas around Sonoita, Patagonia and the San Pedro Valley. And then on into the desert regions of Phoenix, Tucson, Wickenburg and Yuma — the last vestiges of autumn.

Autumn says "Adios" to Arizona and the land rests.

Listening to the sounds of autumn.
Herb and Dorothy McLaughlin

Deep in the sunlit forest.
David Muench

Fall reflections.
   Esther Henderson

September tears.
   Willis Peterson

An autumn corsage
   decorates the rim of the Grand Canyon.
      David Muench

Aspens
in autumn costume.

Willis Peterson

Fall moves in on lower Oak Creek Canyon.

Darwin Van Campen

Autumn lingers below while winter roars over the San Francisco Peaks near Flagstaff.   David Muench

A quiet autumn day on Seven Springs Creek.
Earl Petroff

Winter sneaks in close to the desert.

Richard Jepperson

Up north the winds are less friendly now. They are stronger, for sure, and they bite. They shift from the west to the northwest and finally come roaring out of the north. Skies can become very foreboding.

The leaves are gone now. Plant life is prepared. So is the animal life — coats are thicker, food is stored, and a few hibernate. Other wildlife will move to more hospitable lower elevations.

Then it happens. Snow moves in quietly in the form of a few flurries. But watch out! The skies darken, the winds increase and finally winter matures into a giant. A rancher on the high plateau east of Flagstaff says all snow in his area arrives *horizontally* — with the wind.

Much of the land in these northern and eastern regions sleeps with a blanket of winter. But down on the desert farmers are working with a maturing crop of cotton or cutting hay. Others are harvesting citrus or pecans.

Golfers flock to the Phoenix Open, then to Tucson's Dean Martin Open. Tennis tournaments flourish. Jeep treks across the desert are vogue. Someone says, "Heh, there's snow on Mt. Lemmon!" Tucsonans rush up to the top with skiis, innertubes, sleds; sometimes equipped only with excitement.

It's a grand time in Arizona.

Rushing Oak Creek ignores winter's intrusion.

J. H. Burnett

Through rising mists.
Esther Henderson

A rare blanket of snow in saguaroland.
Tom C. Cooper

So soft and peaceful.   *Chuck Abbott*

Winter lingers in northern Arizona.
Carlos Elmer

Winter pays a visit to the Grand Canyon.   *Esther Henderson*

The following panel —
Arches National Monument, Utah.
David Muench

THE Magazine

Herb and Dorothy McLaughlin

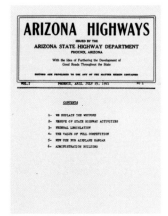

The Pamphlet, 1921

1925

1926

Say two words — Arizona Highways — and ask Americans to identify their meaning. You can expect three out of five, perhaps even a higher ratio, to say something like, "That beautiful Arizona magazine."

Arizona highways are ribbons of asphalt and concrete weaving back and forth across the state. They rank among the finest roads in America and traverse some of the most majestic scenery in the world.

The concept of good scenery and roads had to come together sooner or later. It happened in 1921, as reported in the July 26, 1921, edition of the *Tucson Citizen:* *The first number of "Arizona Highways" was issued yesterday by the state highway department. The front page of publication declares that it is issued "with the idea of furthering the development of good roads throughout the state." Another notice said the magazine would be issued from "time to time" and would be mailed without cost to any taxpayer upon application.*

This first issue contained five sheets of white paper, 8½ by 11 inches, stapled, and with a yellow wraparound cover. The content was entirely typewritten and reproduced by mimeograph or some similar means.

It was a pamphlet, not a magazine, and it lasted roughly eighteen months — nine issues in all.

But it was important, for it was the seed which blossomed into a modern publishing enterprise having yet unmeasured effects upon a state's popularity, growth and development, and upon the magazine industry itself.

Arizona Highways Magazine appeared without much fanfare on April 15, 1925, twenty-eight months after the pamphlet bearing the same name ceased publication. The magazine version amounted to twenty eight pages (no color) and was in every sense a magazine even though it bore absolutely no resemblance to today's version.

Its birth was not an easy one. In order to publish, the Arizona State Highway Department needed authorization from the legislature. There was debate. Solons argued for several weeks about the need,

*Now known as the *Tucson Daily Citizen*.

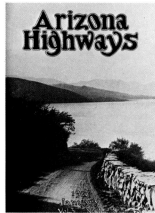

1927

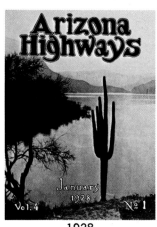

1928

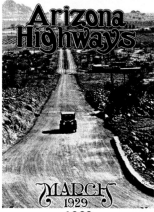

1929

1930

Winter comes to St. John's.

Wayne Davis

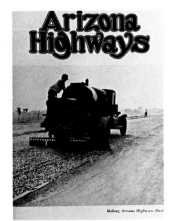

1931

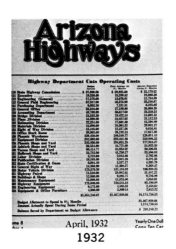

1932

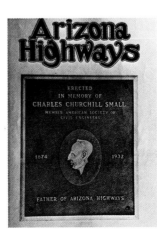

1933

1934

the motives and the cost of producing a magazine promoting Arizona's highways. The press got into the hassle. A 1,000-word editorial in *The Arizona Republican** if March 10, 1925, entitled "The State Highway Magazine" strongly attacked the legislative proposal. One paragraph in particular seems prophetic. It read in part: *Then there is the question of cost. Editors come high. The price of paper is altitudinous, and we expect it to climb even higher. Printers long since ceased working for a song, and the present postal rates are simply a disgrace. Many miles of good roads could be built annually for the cost of producing the State Highway Magazine under the present abnormal conditions of the American dollar being worth only sixty-five cents or thereabouts.*

That was 1925 talk.

Someone in the State Highway Department knew that a highway magazine was an eventuality, for only eighteen days after legislation was approved a new publication came off of the presses. *Arizona Highways*, a real magazine, was born. Circulation was 1,000 copies. That first issue is a true collector's item; there are only a few in libraries, in archives or private collections. It is truly a prized possession, not for its content, its artistic achievements or flowing prose, but because it was the inaugural issue of a publishing phenomenon.

The early issues relied on an editorial diet of highway construction information, financial matters and engineering data. Interspersed were personal items about highway department employees, here and there a joke, road condition reports and some poetry. Each issue contained a "travelogue"—a description of a route (Phoenix to Prescott, etc.) which was a prelude to future content.

It took 15 years before circulation reached 10,000 copies, but things were beginning to happen. From engineering content, the publication was becoming a "see Arizona" magazine. Raymond Carlson arrived in early 1938 as the sixth editor, the same year full-color printing of photographs began with the July cover. Advertising was discontinued, and the magazine was becoming a scenic showpiece. Carlson began the now famous Christmas issue with the December, 1938, edition.

*Now known as *The Arizona Republic*.

1935

1936

1937

1938

Photography was becoming all important. Arizona had to be displayed to attract travelers onto her roads. Carlson was determined to do it.

Even when World War II erupted, Carlson kept up the travel "fever" with invitations to see Arizona's historical and colorful past, and to roam her canyons, deserts and mountains.

1939

Carlson's fervor for the American war effort was almost an obsession. Four months after the attack on Pearl Harbor he used his editorial column to tell Japanese Emperor Hirohito that Arizona's skies were filled with the roar of aircraft because "American boys are learning to fly." He went on, "Trouble is coming for you and your boys, Mr. Hirohito, trouble is coming." On two other occasions, Carlson addressed the Japanese leader directly through his column. The letters were signed with the familiar "R.C.", a signoff that was a Carlson trademark.

Carlson joined the armed forces in 1943. His successor, Bert Campbell, had been editor for a brief period before Carlson in 1937. Campbell continued the Carlson approach, using good photography, historical articles and the "see Arizona" theme.

1940

After the war Carlson returned to Phoenix to his old job. Circulation had increased from 10,000 in 1940 to 70,000 in 1945, despite the ordeals of the war. It exploded as the magazine moved more and more into *color* photography. By 1950 it had reached 165,000 copies.

The sudden rise in circulation in the late 1940s was due not only to Carlson's editorial genius but also to the arrival of James Stevens, a decorated veteran of the war. He was wounded in the South Pacific and while recuperating in a New Guinea hospital saw an issue of *Arizona Highways*. Stevens' hospitalization and that issue helped change the course of the magazine.

1941

Stevens had grown up in Phoenix, and the issue was enough to make him determined to recover and go home. Go home he did, straight to the office of *Arizona Highways*, where Carlson gave him a job in the mailroom. A year later he was named Circulation and Business Manager.

Stevens set out to expand *Arizona Highways'* circulation — first into California, then nationwide, and eventually internationally. Carlson would put the magazine together; Stevens would get it distributed.

Distribution became a highly significant factor. There are those today who flatly state that Arizona's phenomenal development is due to two things: *Arizona Highways* magazine and air conditioning. The theory is that many people and industries would not have been attracted to Arizona if it were not for the magazine. And, once they came to the state, they would not have stayed without air conditioning.

1942

Mission San Xavier del Bac.   *Ray Manley*

1943

1944

1945

For the first 47 years the magazine received a state appropriation to help defray expenses partly resulting from printing of non-revenue producing promotional materials (maps, brochures). Stevens did not ask for the subsidy beginning in 1972. The magazine remains self-supporting today and continues to produce maps and brochures which are distributed free, and maintains other activities to promote state tourism.

The Carlson-Stevens team continued until 1971 when, due to ill health, Carlson retired as editor. He still resides in Phoenix and carries the title Editor Emeritus. Upon Carlson's retirement, Stevens was appointed Director of Publications, and he guides the magazine through its golden anniversary.

Carlson's close editorial colleague during the post-World War II period was George Avey, an artist-designer who meticulously planned the magazine's appearance, pored over tens of thousands of photographs, planned page layouts and closely scrutinized the magazines coming off the presses. Avey retired in 1972 and died in 1973.

Carlson did not leave the editorial reigns to an untested successor. He asked Joseph Stacey to join the staff in 1965 as an editorial assistant. Stacey quickly grasped the Carlson touch, added that of his own, and when the senior editor retired in 1971, Stacey stepped into the lead role and has proven to be an editorial genius in his own right.

In 1973, Stacey and Stevens pushed the average monthly circulation over the half-million mark. In January, 1974, Stacey edited the famous "turquoise issue" an authoritative, majestically illustrated issue on turquoise Indian jewelry. It was sold out in a few days, then was reprinted and reprinted again until more than a million copies were sold. It is a collector's item today, like the first issue forty-nine years earlier.

Stacey's assistant is Wesley Holden. They worked together before joining the magazine. They function as a team; a team much like Carlson and Avey before them.

For more than thirty years, the magazine's editorial content has been the product of two men — not five, ten or twenty as commonly believed. Two men — Carlson and Avey, then Stacey and Holden — have produced the editorial content.

1946

1947

1948

1949

1950

1951

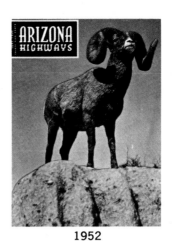

1952

1953

The late George Avey (left) and former editor Raymond Carlson during the 1960s.

Paul Markow

James E. Stevens, director of publications.

1954

1955

1956

1957

Some think the magazine is planned many months ahead, even years in advance. It isn't. Ideas float around, a few plans are formulated, assignments made, and then in a frenzy of editorial brilliance it comes together in a matter of days.

Contributors — writers, photographers and artists — have played a significant role in the magazine's climb to unequaled success. Josef Muench, the dean of contributing photographers, has been a regular for more than thirty-seven years. Esther Henderson began submitting photographs in the late forties. The work of artist Ted DeGrazia first appeared in the magazine in 1943. Photographer Ray Manley attributes his phenomenal photographic career to the publication of his photographs during and immediately after World War II. Manley pays tribute to the magazine: "It changed my entire course of life..."

David Muench, son of Josef, was introduced to editor Carlson at the age of 12. He was invited to submit his first work. The younger Muench is perhaps the most prolific and talented photographer contributing to the magazine on its golden anniversary.

The work of artists Peter Hurd, Olaf Wieghorst, Frederick Remington, Charles M. Russell, Maynard Dixon, and W. R. Leigh; the writing of Joseph Wood Krutch, Frank Waters, Irvin S. Cobb, Ralph Keithley, and Walter Noble Burns have been published.

Artists, writers and photographers have submitted material, not so much for the financial rewards, for the magazine pays modestly for contrfbutions, but for the satisfaction of seeing their creative works reproduced in a quality manner and for the satisfaction of knowing that readers accept and relish their talent.

It also takes a printer to produce a magazine. If it is a prestige magazine, it requires the finest printing talent and technology around. Until 1963, numerous printers, from Los Angeles to San Francisco to Phoenix to Milwaukee, were low bidders in producing the magazine. Black and white pages were printed in one plant, and perhaps two thousand miles away color pages rolled off another press. On occasions the black and white and color sections were assembled in a third city. Then the W. A. Krueger Co. who since 1950 had produced the all-color cover and body sections in Milwaukee, Wisconsin, acquired the

1958

1959

1960

1961

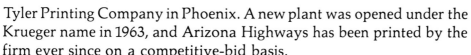

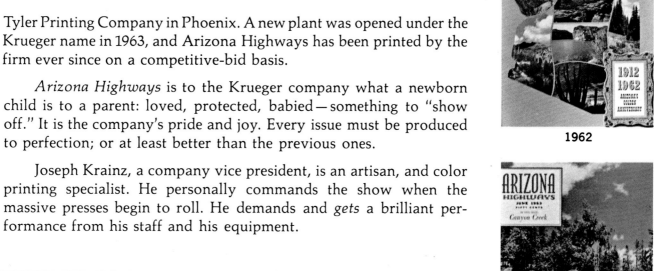
1962

1963

Tyler Printing Company in Phoenix. A new plant was opened under the Krueger name in 1963, and Arizona Highways has been printed by the firm ever since on a competitive-bid basis.

Arizona Highways is to the Krueger company what a newborn child is to a parent: loved, protected, babied—something to "show off." It is the company's pride and joy. Every issue must be produced to perfection; or at least better than the previous ones.

Joseph Krainz, a company vice president, is an artisan, and color printing specialist. He personally commands the show when the massive presses begin to roll. He demands and *gets* a brilliant performance from his staff and his equipment.

The team of editor Joseph Stacey (left) and associate editor Wesley Holden.

Paul Markow

1964

Robert A. Klaus, chairman of the board for the Krueger company, was the initial contact between the magazine and his firm. He continues to play an active role in maintaining the quality of printing and is an avid promoter of *Arizona Highways*.

Gary Avey, Krueger's account manager, and son of the late George Avey, the magazine's art director, has a devotion to the magazine going back to his childhood when his father would bring home pages of the magazine to be designed. The younger Avey is the primary link between his firm and the magazine's editorial and business departments.

The Krueger company, now with several plants nationwide, obviously has been affected by the magazine's content. In 1974 it moved its corporate office from Milwaukee to Scottsdale — perhaps to be closer to the magazine and the scenery which have helped the company achieve prestige.

One knowledgeable about the history of *Arizona Highways* and the magazine publishing business in general must recognize another factor which accounts for some of the publication's success. *Arizona Highways* is a *state*-owned magazine, published by the *state* Department of Transportation. It was founded by the *state* highway department. It always has been a part of the *state* government of Arizona. Yet, politicians have exercised great restraint and wisdom over the years in letting the magazine staff manage its own affairs. Highway department officials have done a magnificent job in constructing Arizona's roads, but have left the magazine business to publishing professionals. That speaks well of both parties. There has been an understanding, a mutual respect — to the benefit of world-wide readers, the magazine itself and the state of Arizona.

Finally, nature and nature's benefactor, The Almighty, have done spectacular things to the state. Arizona has a unique and varied climate, it has scenery unmatched anywhere, fascinating plant and animal life, unsurpassed sunsets and sunrises, intriguing native people, a colorful history, and plenty of places yet to be photographed.

Arizona was created for *Arizona Highways*.

1965

1966

1967

1968

1969

1970

Air-conditioned Arizona.

Carlos Elmer

The following panel —
A view from the Arizona-Sonora Desert Museum.
Herb and Dorothy McLaughlin

1971

1972

1973

1974